My Pets

by Hayley Lee
illustrations by Rick Geary

Harcourt Brace & Company

Orlando Atlanta Austin Boston San Francisco Chicago Dallas New York Toronto London

Have you met my pet Peg?

Peg is in the pen.

Do you see Peg?

Is Peg the cat with
the bell?
No! It is my pet Jen.

Is Peg the jumping dog?

No! It is my pet Zeb.

What is Peg?

Can you tell yet?

Peg likes to peck.
Now I bet you can
tell what Peg is.

Peg is a hen!